OUTDOOR ADVENTURE!
FISHING

Adam G. Klein

ABDO
Publishing Company

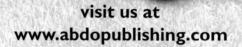

Published by ABDO Publishing Company, 8000 West 78th Street, Edina, Minnesota 55439.
Copyright © 2008 by Abdo Consulting Group, Inc. International copyrights reserved in all
countries. No part of this book may be reproduced in any form without written permission from the
publisher. The Checkerboard Library™ is a trademark and logo of ABDO Publishing Company.

Printed in the United States.

Cover Photo: Getty Images
Interior Photos: Alamy pp. 8, 13; Comstock pp. 11, 15; Corbis pp. 16, 25, 28;
    Getty Images pp. 1, 19, 21, 27; Index Stock p. 5; iStockphoto pp. 7, 10, 11, 14, 20, 22, 26;
    Neil Klinepier pp. 17, 18; Peter Arnold pp. 9, 11, 23; U.S. Fish and Wildlife Service pp. 10, 11

Series Coordinator: Rochelle Baltzer
Editors: Rochelle Baltzer, BreAnn Rumsch
Art Direction & Cover Design: Neil Klinepier

Library of Congress Cataloging-in-Publication Data

Klein, Adam G., 1976-
 Fishing / Adam G. Klein.
    p. cm. -- (Outdoor adventure!)
 Includes index.
 ISBN 978-1-59928-958-8
 1. Fishing--Juvenile literature. I. Title.

 SH445.K485 2008
 799.1--dc22

                    2007029166

CONTENTS

SEA BOUND

Jason had not felt this great in a long time. The salty breeze cleared his nose. The bright sun stung his skin. Boating on the ocean waves was better than he had ever imagined.

Suddenly, something caught Jason's eye. A dark, silvery fish leaped out of the water and arched its back. It appeared to pause for just a moment before falling back into the ocean. Its bladelike tail was last to disappear into the rolling water. Jason and his father watched in astonishment.

"Swordfish," said a gruff voice from behind them. Jason turned to see the gray-haired captain pulling off her stocking cap. "It's amazing every time I see them jump like that." She stared into the sea for a moment before looking back at Jason. "I've got a rod in my cabin. Beautiful days like this shouldn't go to waste."

So, Jason grabbed the rod and cast his line into the sparkling water. His father stood next to him, as Jason awaited the challenge that every angler hopes for.

Swordfish live in mild to tropical ocean temperatures. They can swim at speeds of up to 60 miles per hour (100 km/h)!

WHY FISH?

Fishing is a popular hobby. Every year, more than 44 million Americans over the age of six go fishing. But, fishing was not always only a hobby. People began fishing as a way to obtain food for survival. Throughout the years, it has also become a recreational activity.

There are many ways to fish. Anglers often fish while standing on a dock, on a shoreline, or in a stream. Fishing is relaxing for those who wish to spend time alone. Yet, it can also be a lively group activity. People can cast a line during an afternoon trip to a nearby lake. Or, they can **embark** on a weeklong fishing voyage aboard a **chartered** boat.

Anglers practice their sport for various reasons. Some prefer the peaceful experience of casting on quiet waters. Others **crave** the excitement of pulling in **trophy** fish.

Fishing is also an enjoyable way to exercise. Regular exercise helps strengthen the body. And, spending time near water and in fresh air is a good way to relieve **stress**. No matter the reason, fishing is a great activity!

Eighty-eight percent of Americans have fished at least once in their lives.

WATER TYPES

Different kinds of water are home to different kinds of fish. Freshwater and salt water are the two main types of water. Lakes, ponds, streams, rivers, and swamps are filled with freshwater. Fish such as perch and walleyes live in these places. Certain types of bass and catfish also live in freshwater.

The ocean is made of salt water. The largest fish species live in salt water. Sharks, halibut, swordfish, and tuna are saltwater fish. These fish are often taken as **trophies**. Fighting against a large fish and pulling it in can be an exciting challenge!

Estuaries make up yet another type of water. When a river reaches an ocean, salt

Chesapeake Bay is the largest estuary in the United States. It receives salt water from the Atlantic Ocean and freshwater from more than 50 rivers and streams.

water mixes with freshwater. An estuary is the special **environment** that forms there.

In estuaries, the constant mixing of water traps plant **nutrients**. This provides a favorable home for animals such as oysters and clams. Estuaries are also important nursery areas for some fish.

Both male and female sockeye salmon turn a deep red color before spawning. Long, hook-shaped jaws and a humped back indicate a spawning male.

ADAPTABLE FISH

Not many fish can survive in both freshwater and salt water. However, certain fish species have bodies that allow them to travel between the two types of water. Anadromous (uh-NA-druh-muhs) fish live in salt water but spawn, or reproduce, in freshwater. Catadromous (kuh-TA-druh-muhs) fish live in freshwater but spawn in salt water.

Sockeye salmon are anadromous. After hatching in either shallow streams or lakeshores, they spend up to three years in freshwater. Young salmon gradually move to deeper water. During this time, their bodies change to prepare for living in salt water. They turn a silvery color to match their upcoming environment. Their kidneys and gills also change to process salt water. Finally, the salmon venture into the ocean.

Most sockeye salmon spend two years in the ocean. Then, they make the difficult journey upriver to spawn. Amazingly, they return to the same area they were born in! Sockeye salmon die within a few weeks after spawning. And, new eggs begin the cycle yet again.

A FRESHWATER FISH'S HOME

To be a successful angler, you must know about fish habitats. Water depth, temperature, and ground cover affect where certain types of fish reside. Some fish prefer warm, shallow water. Others thrive in cool, deep water.

Smaller fish, such as sunfish and perch, hide in weedy areas for protection. Larger predator fish often wait outside of weeds to catch stray fish. Other good places to catch fish are near rocky areas or under docks or fallen trees.

Walleyes prefer gravel, rock, or firm sand bottoms. They use sunken trees as cover and as feeding sites.

Muskellunge, or muskies, *(right)* prefer cool water. They lurk in weed beds to wait for prey, such as yellow perch *(below)*.

THE ROLE OF OXYGEN

Just like humans, fish need oxygen to survive. But instead of breathing air, fish breathe water. Different types of water contain different amounts of oxygen. Oxygen levels affect where certain fish can be found. These levels increase if there are many plants or a lot of movement between the water and the air.

The constant flow of water in rivers and waterfalls keeps oxygen levels high. Certain types of fish, such as trout, prefer these places.

Waters with low oxygen are home to other kinds of fish, such as carp. These areas include slow-moving streams, murky swamps, and still lakes. Carp can even thrive in polluted water.

FISH BIOLOGY

Understanding fish behavior is necessary for anglers. Just like humans, fish use their senses to explore their surroundings. Fish are attracted to certain smells and sights. But they are easily **repelled**, too. If fish sense something that makes them nervous, they flee.

Fish have an excellent sense of smell. They are often drawn toward certain scents. This helps them locate food. Fish are also very sensitive to noise. They may be curious about something they hear. However, boat motors and loud voices easily scare them away. So, it is important for anglers to stay quiet on the water.

Fish cannot see very far, but they have a good range of vision. This helps them navigate. Some fish can see colors. So, anglers often use brightly colored bait to attract fish. Some people believe red is the most attractive color to fish. However, fish can only see red at close distances. In deep water, blue and purple are most visible.

Fish have an additional sensory organ called the lateral line, which runs down their sides. The lateral line acts as a sense for both hearing and touch. It detects vibrations as well as changes in water temperature and pressure. The lateral line also helps fish keep their balance!

The lateral line helps fish escape from predators, locate prey, and stay in schools.

TRICKING FISH

Anglers use bait to fool fish into thinking they will get a meal. Some fish are attracted to live bait, such as minnows, worms, salamanders, frogs, and grubs. Others are attracted to foods such as cheese or corn.

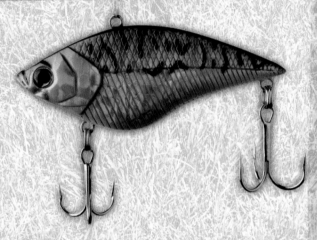

Many fish go after fish-shaped lures. But, some freshwater fish will eat popcorn and marshmallows!

Using artificial bait, or lures, is also a popular way to attract fish. A spinner is a widely used type of artificial bait. It is a rounded piece of metal that twirls in the water. Many fish are attracted to the movement of the shiny metal. Their curiosity leads them to strike the swirling spinners. Other kinds of lures include plugs, spoons, and jigs.

Fly fishers use a type of artificial bait called a fly. An artificial fly resembles a real fly or other insect. It consists

TIP *A spoon lure is ideal when fishing for northern pike. It is made of thin metal and resembles a spoon.*

of a small hook disguised with a colorful, hairlike covering. Fly fishers cast into rivers, where the current carries the fly. It takes much practice to master the art of fly-fishing. Still, this challenge appeals to many anglers.

Fly-fishing is one of the oldest fishing methods. It has a different style from bait fishing. Instead of using a rod to cast bait, fly fishers use the weight of line to cast a fly.

TACKLE

Fishing equipment is called tackle. Your choice of tackle depends on where and how you plan to fish. Freshwater and saltwater tackle differ. And, freshwater tackle varies among fishing methods. For example, bait fishing and fly-fishing require different tackle.

However, there are some basic items that an angler should carry along in any situation. Basic tackle includes hooks, fishing pliers, knives, weights, lures, line, and a net. Most of these items can be organized and stored in a tackle box. That way, they are easy to transport.

Waders have specially designed soles that give anglers secure footing on slippery surfaces.

Certain situations call for different types of fishing equipment. In a boat, a life jacket should be worn at all times for safety.

When fishing in streams, some anglers wear waders or rubber boots. Waders are long rubber pants that fit over clothing to keep the body warm and dry. They are ideal when fishing in cold water. However, anglers must be careful not to fall because waders can quickly fill with water.

TACKLE BOX TREASURES

The contents of a tackle box vary, depending on specific fishing conditions. But, there are some basic items that every angler should have in a tackle box.

- hooks
- lures
- weights
- bobbers
- line
- fishing pliers
- filet knife
- gloves
- cotton cloths
- bandages
- sunglasses
- sunscreen
- insect repellent

RODS AND REELS

Fishing rods were traditionally made of wood or bamboo. **Fiberglass**, **carbon fiber**, and **graphite** are the common rod materials today.

There are many types of fishing rods to choose from. Your choice depends on the type of fishing you plan to do. Long rods cast farther, while shorter rods are easier to use in tight situations. Longer, **flexible** rods are ideal for catching large fish. Modern fishing rods for adults generally range from 5 to 15 feet (2 to 5 m) long.

After choosing a rod, you must match it with a reel. Fishing reels store and release line. Most

Spinning reels are also called open-faced reels. The U-shaped piece rotates around the reel to take in line.

reels can control the **tension** of the line while catching a fish.

The two most popular types of reels are spinning reels and spin-casting reels. These are also the easiest to use. When casting with a spin-cast reel, an angler pushes a button to release line.

Choosing fishing line is the next step. Line is measured in pounds equal to the amount of pressure it would take to break the line. Lightweight line is ideal for catching small fish because it moves easily through the water. Heavier line is stronger and should be used if large fish are in the area.

Another type of line is used for fly-fishing. Fly-fishing line has various thicknesses. That way, the artificial fly can reach different depths in the water.

Spinning reels work well in both salt water and freshwater. Some saltwater models hold a large amount of line. This is helpful when reeling in strong fish that don't give up easily!

BOATS AND TOOLS

Many people prefer to fish from boats. Some anglers enjoy the peace and quiet that fishing in a canoe offers. Yet, others might like the thrill of casting from a 26-foot (8-m) boat on the Great Lakes or the ocean.

A GPS can help an angler locate a promising fishing spot. It can also track previously identified sites.

In boats, some people use high-tech equipment to navigate and to locate fish. They might use a Global Positioning System (GPS). This tracking device uses **satellites** to determine an angler's exact location. A depth finder is another helpful tool. This instrument uses **sonar** technology to read water depth and to locate fish.

TIP *Before trolling, check local rules for the area you plan to fish in. Trolling is not allowed in all places.*

Another popular fishing tool is called a downrigger. It allows anglers to keep bait in deep water while **trolling**. This system uses a small ball that is attached to fishing line with a clip. A **winch** is connected to the ball, so an angler can raise or lower the line. When a fish strikes the hook, the clip releases line so the fish can be reeled in.

Some depth finders can show a tiny jig bouncing around 30 feet (9 m) under a boat!

ICE FISHING

Even in the deepest chill of winter, there are fishing opportunities. Fish are less active in cold water, but they still bite at food. Ice fishing is a favorite cold-weather activity of many devoted anglers.

To stay warm, many ice anglers sit inside small structures called fish houses. A fish house is towed onto thick ice.

Anglers use these temporary structures throughout the winter. They bring them ashore before the ice melts in the spring.

Ice fishing requires special procedures. An angler must cut a hole through the ice to reach water. This can be done using a drill or a knife. It is important to slowly and quietly cut the hole. Loud noises on the ice will scare away nearby fish.

Ice fishing also requires special equipment. A typical ice fishing pole is about three feet (1 m) long. A bobber, weights, and a hook are attached to the line. The bobber rests on the water's surface. The weights carry the hook to its desired depth.

When a fish strikes the hook, the bobber dips under the surface. This means it is time to work. To set the hook in place, anglers slightly pull up the rod. Then, they reel in their catch!

Ice should be at least 4 inches (10 cm) thick to be safe for walking. It should be 8 to 12 inches (20 to 30 cm) thick for an automobile and 12 to 15 inches (30 to 38 cm) thick for a truck. But in early winter, these numbers should be doubled to be safe.

HANDLING FISH

Pulling a fish out of the water is exciting. But, handling it can be tricky. Many fish have sharp fins or teeth. So, anglers need to protect themselves. Just the same, fish must be protected from people.

The scales of most fish are covered in a protective slime. The slime creates a barrier that **bacteria** cannot pass through. This prevents fish from getting infections on their bodies.

Anglers should always handle their catch with wet hands to protect fish scales. Some anglers prefer to wear gloves when handling fish. However, gloves remove more of the protective slime than bare hands do. Using a net is another option. This way, an angler does not have to touch the fish at all.

A fish's gills and eyes can also be easily damaged if they are handled incorrectly. Severe damage to a fish's gills could kill it. So when removing a hook from a fish, make sure to not touch its gills.

Using a net to land a fish is quicker than using your hand. Therefore, fish don't get as tired and are more likely to survive after being released.

If you plan to release your catch, place it back into the water as soon as you remove the hook. Some fish species cannot be outside of water for long. Fair-**game** anglers make sure to give their catch the best possible chance of survival.

A FRESH CATCH

Experienced anglers and fishing professionals often catch and release fish. They remember large **trophy** fish by an image. Some catch-and-release anglers take a photograph as soon as they catch a fish. Then, they immediately release the fish back into the water.

Catch-and-release fishing is good for the **environment**. Released fish can reproduce and therefore increase fish populations. This ensures that plenty of fish will be available to catch in the future.

However, eating a freshly caught fish can be a yummy reward after a day on the water. If anglers choose to keep their catch, they must make sure the fish stay fresh.

Anglers can carry their catch in creels worn on the back or slung over the shoulder.

There are a couple of ways to keep fish fresh before eating them. Fish can stay in water on special hooks called stringers. Or, they can be stored in a basket called a creel. On land, fish should be immediately placed on ice and prepared as soon as possible. This way, fish remain fresh and tasty.

If you plan to release your catch, gently ease it back into the water. Move it back and forth to run water across its gills until it can swim away. Never throw a fish back into the water.

FISHING RULES

Overfishing threatens the **environment**. Therefore, state governments set limits for how many fish can be taken in one day. Other laws are in effect during certain times of the year. For example, fish do not reproduce if they are **disturbed** during their breeding months.

To ensure there are plenty of fish to catch, it is important to learn and follow fishing laws. Some laws prevent illegal fishing methods, such as shocking fish or trapping them in illegal areas. The use of harmful hooks and damaging nets are against the law, too.

To fish legally, one must also obtain a fishing license. This can be purchased from the Department of Natural Resources in your state. People can also buy them at sporting goods stores or bait shops, as well as online.

Purchasing a fishing license helps the **environment**. Money from licenses is put toward restoring **habitats**, restocking fish, and keeping public spaces open. Together, fishing licenses, stamps, tags, and permits generated about $600 million in 2001!

Like Jason discovered, spending a sunny day on the water can be an incredible experience. Sitting in a cold shack over an ice hole can be fun, too! Once you know the basics, fishing is easy. No matter what happens, have fun out there. And, good luck catching your next big fish!

A day spent fishing is a great way to relax and enjoy nature. Getting outside in breezy, fresh air is good for your health, too!

GLOSSARY

bacteria - tiny, one-celled organisms that can only be seen through a microscope.

carbon fiber - a very strong lightweight synthetic, or artificially made, fiber.

chartered - hired, rented, or leased usually for private use.

crave - to strongly desire.

disturb - to interfere with or interrupt.

embark - to make a start.

environment - all the surroundings that affect the growth and well-being of a living thing.

fiberglass - glass in fibrous form used for making various products.

flexible - able to bend or move easily.

game - wild animals hunted for food or sport.

graphite - a soft, shiny black form of carbon.

habitat - a place where a living thing is naturally found.

nutrient - a substance found in food and used in the body to promote growth, maintenance, and repair.

repel - to drive away.

satellite - a manufactured object that orbits Earth.

sonar - a device for detecting the presence and location of objects underwater by using sound waves.

stress - a physical, chemical, or emotional factor that causes bodily or mental unrest and may be involved in causing some diseases.

tension - pressure caused by the action of a pulling force.

troll - to fish by trailing a lure or a baited hook through the water from a moving boat.

trophy - a game animal or fish suitable for mounting.

winch - a machine that has a roller on which a rope, a cable, or a chain is wound for pulling or lifting.

WEB SITES

To learn more about fishing, visit ABDO Publishing Company on the World Wide Web at www.abdopublishing.com. Web sites about fishing are featured on our Book Link.s page. These links are routinely monitored and updated to provide the most current information available.

INDEX